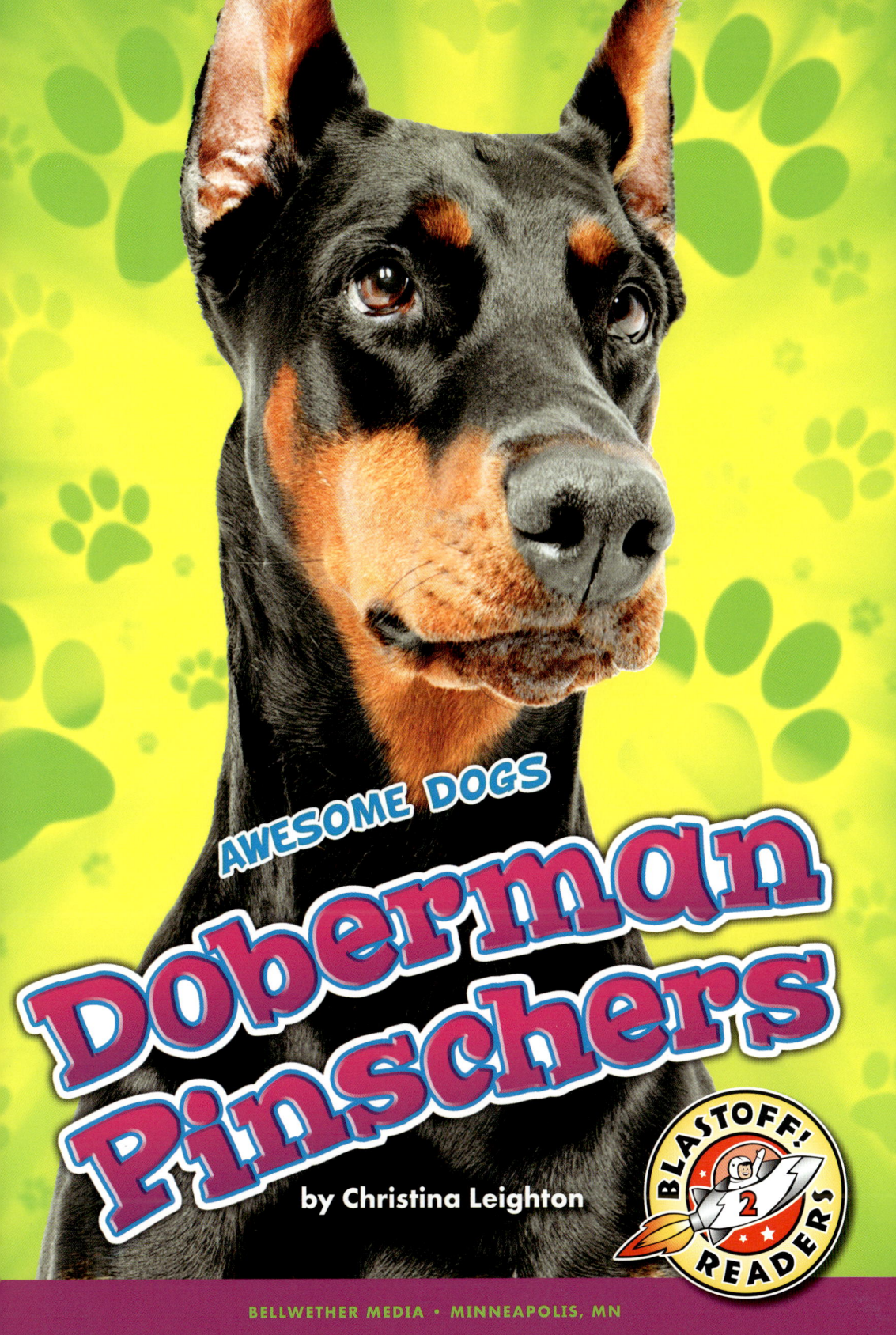

AWESOME DOGS

Doberman Pinschers

by Christina Leighton

BLASTOFF! READERS 2

BELLWETHER MEDIA • MINNEAPOLIS, MN

Note to Librarians, Teachers, and Parents:

Blastoff! Readers are carefully developed by literacy experts and combine standards-based content with developmentally appropriate text.

Level 1 provides the most support through repetition of high-frequency words, light text, predictable sentence patterns, and strong visual support.

Level 2 offers early readers a bit more challenge through varied simple sentences, increased text load, and less repetition of high-frequency words.

Level 3 advances early-fluent readers toward fluency through increased text and concept load, less reliance on visuals, longer sentences, and more literary language.

Level 4 builds reading stamina by providing more text per page, increased use of punctuation, greater variation in sentence patterns, and increasingly challenging vocabulary.

Level 5 encourages children to move from "learning to read" to "reading to learn" by providing even more text, varied writing styles, and less familiar topics.

Whichever book is right for your reader, Blastoff! Readers are the perfect books to build confidence and encourage a love of reading that will last a lifetime!

This edition first published in 2017 by Bellwether Media, Inc.

No part of this publication may be reproduced in whole or in part without written permission of the publisher. For information regarding permission, write to Bellwether Media, Inc., Attention: Permissions Department, 5357 Penn Avenue South, Minneapolis, MN 55419.

Library of Congress Cataloging-in-Publication Data

Names: Leighton, Christina, author.
Title: Doberman Pinschers / by Christina Leighton.
Other titles: Blastoff! Readers. 2, Awesome Dogs.
Description: Minneapolis, MN : Bellwether Media, Inc., [2017] | Series: Blastoff! Readers. Awesome Dogs | Audience: Ages 5-8. | Audience: K to grade 3. | Includes bibliographical references and index.
Identifiers: LCCN 2015047022 | ISBN 9781626173927 (hardcover : alk. paper)
Subjects: LCSH: Doberman pinscher–Juvenile literature. | Dog breeds–Juvenile literature.
Classification: LCC SF429.D6 L45 2017 | DDC 636.73/6–dc23
LC record available at http://lccn.loc.gov/2015047022

Text copyright © 2017 by Bellwether Media, Inc. BLASTOFF! READERS and associated logos are trademarks and/or registered trademarks of Bellwether Media, Inc. SCHOLASTIC, CHILDREN'S PRESS, and associated logos are trademarks and/or registered trademarks of Scholastic Inc.

Printed in the United States of America, North Mankato, MN.

Table of Contents

What Are Doberman Pinschers?	4
Shiny Coats and Colors	8
History of Doberman Pinschers	12
Loving Protectors	18
Glossary	22
To Learn More	23
Index	24

What Are Doberman Pinschers?

Doberman pinschers are **alert** dogs. The **breed** is known to be brave and strong.

The dogs are called Dobies for short.

Dobies have deep, **broad** chests. Their heads are long and narrow.

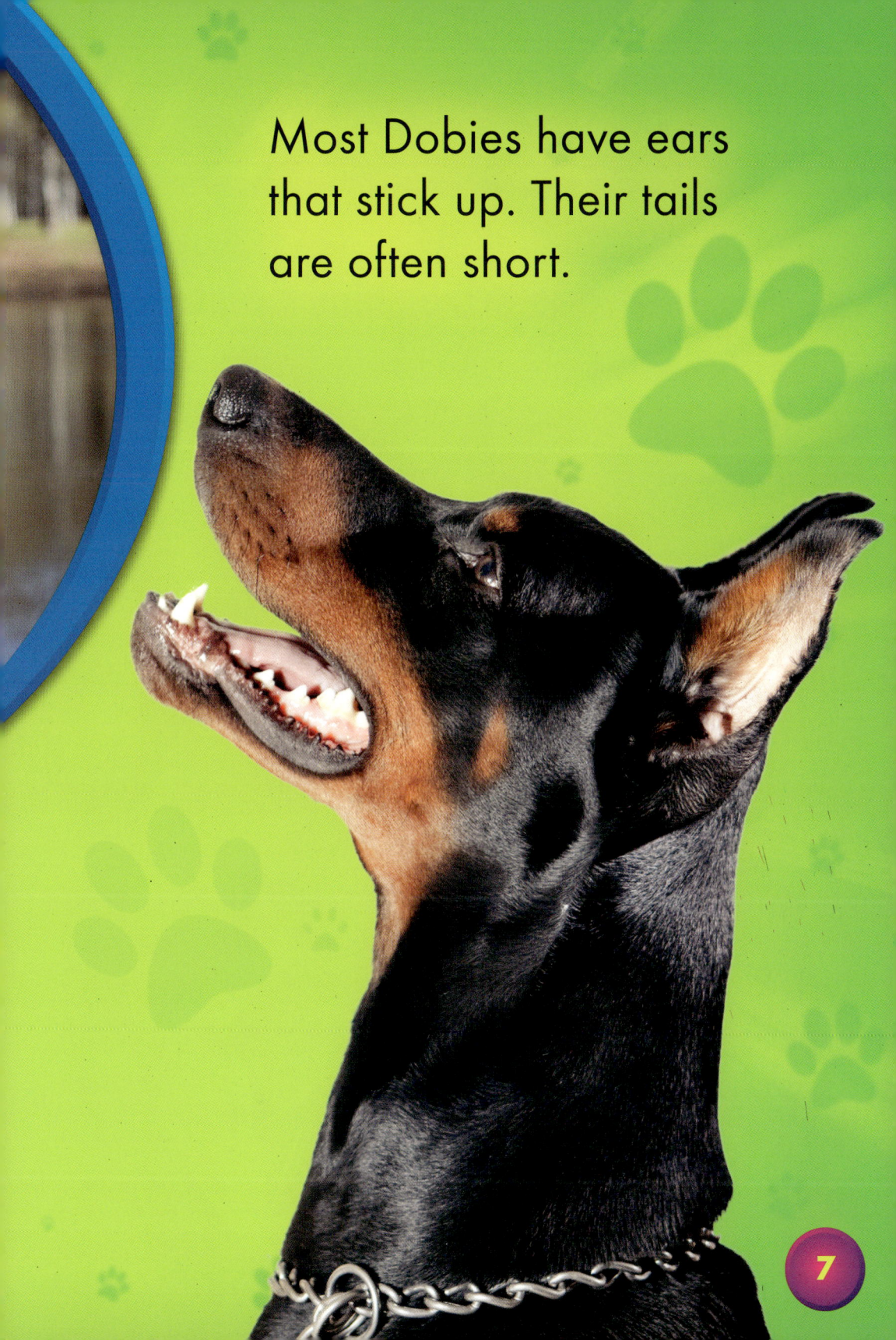

Most Dobies have ears that stick up. Their tails are often short.

Shiny Coats and Colors

These dogs have shiny **coats**.

Their short hairs grow close together. This makes their fur thick and smooth.

black

Dobie coats are black, blue, red, or **fawn**.

Doberman Pinscher Coats

blue   red   fawn

Tan markings often appear on their chins, chests, and legs. Most have dots above their eyes.

History of Doberman Pinschers

The breed began in Germany around 1890. The first Dobie was **bred** by Louis Dobermann.

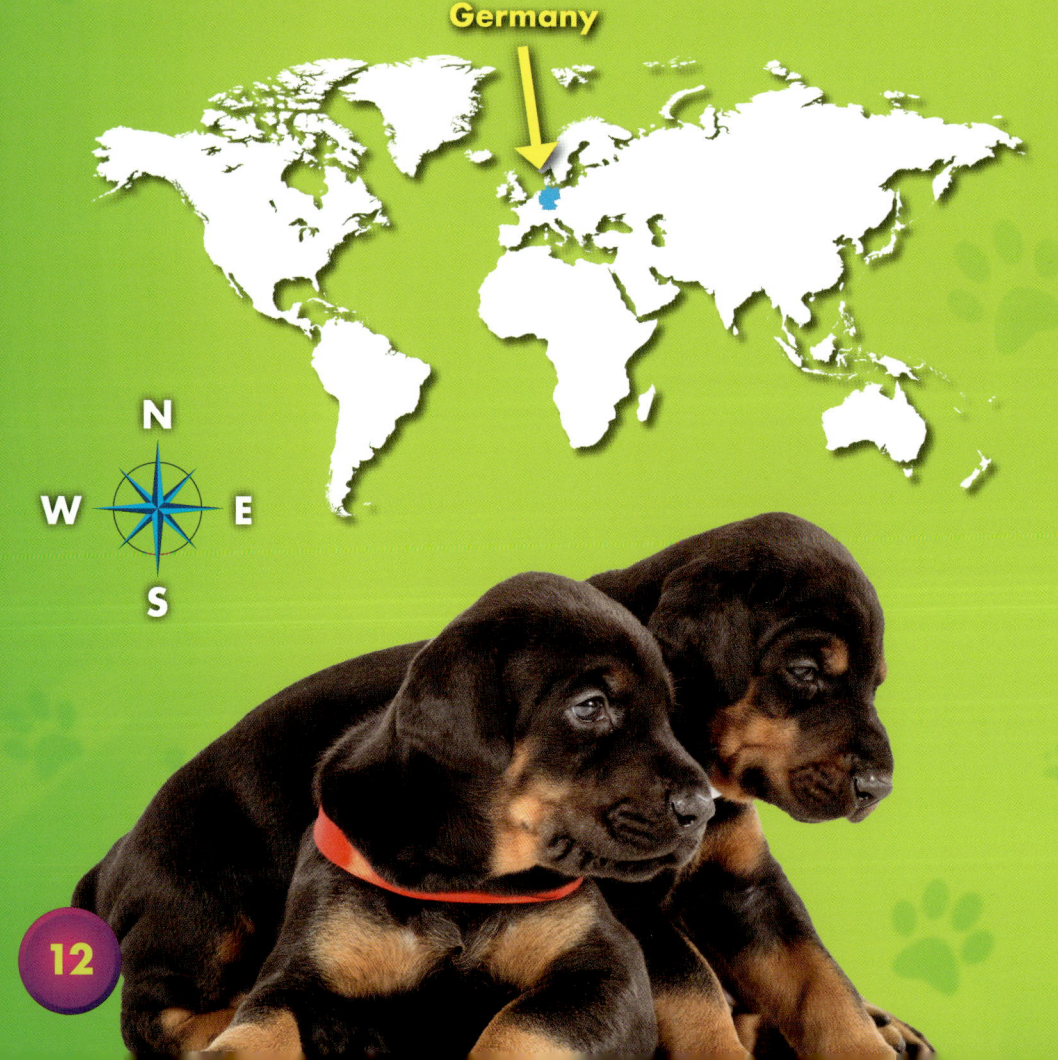

He needed a dog to **protect** him while he worked as a tax collector.

United States Marines with Doberman pinscher, 1944

In World War II, Dobies served on battlefields. They warned soldiers of danger.

A **statue** named "Always Faithful" honors these war dogs. It stands where they served.

Today, some Dobies still work with the military. Others work with **search and rescue** teams.

The dogs are in the **Working Group** of the **American Kennel Club**.

Loving Protectors

These medium-sized dogs have a lot of energy.

Owners need to train and play with Dobies often.

Doberman pinschers are tough dogs. But they are also loving and **loyal**.

They keep their families safe!

Glossary

alert—quick to notice or act

American Kennel Club—an organization that keeps track of dog breeds in the United States

bred—purposely mated two dogs to make puppies with certain qualities

breed—a type of dog

broad—wide

coats—the hair or fur covering some animals

fawn—a light brown color

loyal—having constant support for someone

protect—to keep safe

search and rescue—teams that look for and help people in danger

statue—a figure made from stone, metal, or some other material

Working Group—a group of dog breeds that have a history of performing jobs for people

To Learn More

AT THE LIBRARY
Johnson, Jinny. *Doberman Pinscher.* Mankato, Minn.: Smart Apple Media, 2015.

Patent, Dorothy Hinshaw. *Dogs on Duty: Soldiers' Best Friends on the Battlefield and Beyond.* New York, N.Y.: Walker & Co., 2012.

Petrie, Kristin. *Doberman Pinschers.* Minneapolis, Minn.: ABDO Publishing Company, 2014.

ON THE WEB
Learning more about Doberman pinschers is as easy as 1, 2, 3.

1. Go to www.factsurfer.com.

2. Enter "Doberman pinschers" into the search box.

3. Click the "Surf" button and you will see a list of related web sites.

With factsurfer.com, finding more information is just a click away.

Index

"Always Faithful" (statue), 15
American Kennel Club, 17
battlefields, 14
bred, 12
breed, 4, 12
chests, 6, 11, 17
chins, 11
coats, 8, 10, 11, 17
colors, 10, 11
Dobermann, Louis, 12
ears, 7
energy, 18
eyes, 11
families, 21
fur, 9
Germany, 12
hairs, 9
heads, 6, 17
legs, 11
life span, 17
markings, 11
military, 16
name, 5
owners, 19
play, 19
protect, 13
search and rescue, 16
size, 18
soldiers, 14
tails, 7
trainability, 17, 19
war dogs, 15
work, 16
Working Group, 17
World War II, 14

The images in this book are reproduced through the courtesy of: Dmytro Zinkevych, front cover, p. 20; jocic, p. 4; DragoNika, pp. 5, 10-11; dezi, p. 6; viki2win, p. 7; Fotokostic, p. 8; anetapics, p. 9; J. Harrison/ Kimball Stock, p. 11; Pavel Shlykov, p. 12; PushAnn, p. 13; Bettmann/ Corbis, p. 14; Photri/ Topham/ The Image Works, p. 15; Tierfotoagentur/ N. Noack/ Alamy, pp. 16 (subject), 19; S_Photo, p. 16 (background); tugolukof, p. 17; Denisa Doudova, p. 18; Myphototime, p. 21.